This Book

was written

by a

LOCAL AUTHOR

Pitt Poetry Series
Ed Ochester, Editor

Tiger Heron

Robin Becker

UNIVERSITY OF PITTSBURGH PRESS

Published by the University of Pittsburgh Press, Pittsburgh, Pa., 15260

Copyright © 2014, Robin Becker

Manufactured in the United States of America

Printed on acid-free paper

10 9 8 7 6 5 4 3 2 1

ISBN 13: 978-0-8229-6298-4

ISBN 10: 0-8229-6298-5

For my family of friends
and
in memory of my parents:

Anne Dee Becker (March 23, 1921–November 3, 2006)
Benjamin Bruce Becker (October 29, 1920–February 23, 2010)

Contents

III

I

Prairie Dogs

for Khyber Oser
and in memory of Matthew Shepard (1976–1998)

They tenanted the far high school field,
the dispossessed Lotaburger lot, the dog run.
Shifty, sometimes rabid, they dared to stand

upright, almost human, and stare. I feared their deft
hands, the shrug of shoulders before they spiraled
underground. That day one hung panting on a twist

of barbed wire; front paws scored the dirt.
A ripped haunch, roiling and bloody, flashed,
and I turned away, yanking the dog behind me,

when my young cousin whispered *what's
this*, and groped for a stick to free the leg,
and when that didn't work, he knelt in the trashy

run, his face close to the scrabbler, fingers
plying the greasy, furred gash, the entrails
glazed with flies which might have deterred

someone else, but he sat, now cross-legged,
unwinding the wrecked limb the way the hands
that lifted the boy in Wyoming must have worked.

To A Poet
for Maxine Kumin

You never found comfort in doctrine
        but in the winter
coats of your horses and in the climbing

        tendrils of your beans
all making their way into the strict lines
        to which I now return

You set the cool spring trail ride on Amanda
        alongside the slaughterer's
bullet slamming sidelong

        You set the body
swimming in the pond, mind dissolving
        and shucking off its burden

You let the woman lie down with the bear
        and migrate
with the arctic caribou Your anguish

        in aligning loss
with love became metrical protests
        as a gorgeous May

afternoon enters every window of the house
        where someone is sick
and someone is reading to the sick

        and someone makes supper using
every language available to say *nourishment,*
        mystery, wisdom,

and *I will sleep on the floor in your room*

Hospice

I wanted to believe in it, the word
softer than *hospital* but still not *home*—

like any other frame house on the street,
it had a lawn, a door, a bell—

inside, our friend lay, a view
of the garden from her room but no lift

to raise her from the bed. A sword,
the sun plunged across the cotton blankets.

I wanted dying to be Mediterranean,
curated, a villa, like the Greek sanatoria

where the ancients cared for their sick
on airy porticos and verandas

with stone paths that led to libraries.
A nurse entered her room and closed the door.

For the alleviation of pain, I praise
Morpheus, god of dreams, unlocking

the medicine drawer with a simple key,
narcotic placed beneath the tongue.

In the hall, the volunteer offered us coffee.
How could I think the Mozart in G major

we played to distract her could distract her?
Or marble sculpture in the atrium?

A Last Go

My mother takes the world into her mouth,
she takes the sour-cream coffee cake and
the *rugelach* with walnuts and currants.
She wants a pecan raisin loaf, two loaves,
See's suckers, and *mandelbrodt,*
and I'll take her hunger any way I can,
mainlining my mother's desires, finding
in her appetites the young woman—
tortoise-shell sunglasses and dark hair
pulled back in a silk scarf—
who gunned the white Ford Galaxy, hardtop
convertible, a ringer for Jackie O.
This is her reward for years
of tuning deprivation
like a violin, of learning to do more on less
and less until she lived on argument, solo
performance, dry toast and black coffee, the fish
dish halved. Now that medical studies show
the skinny live longer, she's gained
the sweet taste of being right all along.
Go ahead, Ma, try the ginger scones,
the lemon poppy seed cake.
All the hours you hoarded have turned
into years; there's time for a last
go at pleasure.

Modern Death

"You'll miss me and I'll miss you. Let me sleep," she said.
I badgered the corridors, begging advice.
Father watched TV, vigorously, by her bed.

Nurses urged paper cups of colored meds,
but she took only painkillers they spliced.
"You'll miss me and I'll miss you. Let me sleep," she said

and drifted off. I panicked in the dreadful
state of Florida at death's imprecise
approach. Father watched TV, vigorously, by her bed,

while I questioned strangers: Bring her home, instead?
"No!" Father wept when I spoke of hospice.
"You'll miss me and I'll miss you. Let me sleep," she said.

The failure of the pacemaker led
to technicians disconnecting the device.
Father watched TV, vigorously, by her bed.

"Why am I alive when I want to be dead?"
my mother moaned, articulate, concise.
"You'll miss me and I'll miss you. Let me sleep," she said.
Father watched TV, vigorously, by her bed.

Post Time

What my father loved about the track—
time compressed into three-minute segments,
the idea of someone losing his shirt
or a few bucks, or winning big . . .

He loved the last-minute window,
gamblers tense to place the last winning bet,
and all the losing tickets he stepped on
walking to the boy who ran to get his car.

Once, at ten, sleepless, I carried to his room
some nameless fear I wanted him to soothe.
He told me his secret: to lie on one side
and concentrate to keep away the dread.

I used to think only of my father's anger.
Now I think of his loneliness.

Storm King Sculpture Park

We circled
    fabricated girders,
    welded, hoisted,
their surfaces scored.

Around us, a meadow marked
    and pierced
    with immense
human effort. You spoke

first of our terse
    formality
    with each other
after months of silence,

the strain of polite gestures.
    How had we arrived
    at this wide, quiet place
with so much to name?

The sculptures enlisted us,
    became us,
    steel-limbed sieves
through which a few names poured—

Goldsworthy,
    di Suvero, Smith—
    and then stopped,
grit in the colander.

Kouros

We found the stone man lying in a ditch
a short walk from the harbor with its flags
and identical sidewalk *tavernas*.
His torso stretched two stories down the slope,
his stone beard mimicked the shape of the bay,
where a woman beat goatskin on rocks,
slapping and pounding as the surf banged in.
They say the carvers left him where he lay,
too heavy to move; we sat beside his
broken hands and sunken eyes. At the quay,
the woman thrashed flensed skin on stone.

Herself

If she falls down the cellar steps carrying her laundry
I'll be one of those impossible friends who says
She never listens to a word I say, I said I'd carry
the laundry down. Having given up
her car, she will not give up washer and dryer,
hot and cold, the small, medium, and large decisions
she takes with dials in the stone basement.
Rat terrier, I sulk by the exhaust.
She stacks clothes into her backpack and hoists
herself up the narrow steps by the spindly rail, swaying
backward, toward me, two steps below.
If she tumbles, I'll catch her, stubborn—
when into my arms, the delicate and permanent press.

Late June Owl

They say it's a bad
summer for ticks, a good summer
for day lilies

(Quality Control likes
to measure and evaluate
with continuous monitoring)

They say my friend
has a few weeks, maybe a month
but you never know

As the raptor people know
how to keep the orphaned
screech owl before release

may his keepers
open the airy nets of their patience
when he tries them

They say the screech owl's trill
has more than four
individual calls per second

They say they can
barely hear his voice, more like wind
than words

They say the owlet will leave
the open cage when fully flighted
and capable of hunting

They say the dying
will sometimes wait until everyone
has left the room

Old Florida

When the soon-to-be famous hurricane
hurried to their neighborhood, I begged them

to leave. Rain made a cassoulet of the parking lot;
winds juggled giant palms like rolling pins;

shy herons took cover beneath awnings
and stood like museum guards in doorways—

but my parents hunkered down, children
under desks in the '50s, the storm their personal blitz.

I cried, I screamed over the phone but they rejected
the generator-backed shelter I found, chose canned

goods and bunker, until the phone died—and I consigned them
to their neighbors, their luck, their blood thinners.

Eighty-seven years old, they hid on the ninth floor,
elevator out, infrastructure crumbling, but more

than death or thirst they feared their daughter
with her talk of evacuation.

Leaving home, even for natural disaster, made them
refugees, registrants in a vast and subtly

documented conspiracy to remove them
from their apartment to assisted living.

Neighbors found them sweating in their foxhole,
ferried batteries, salami, and ice,

and when the power came back, they phoned
    to report that hardship brought out the kindness

    in people, wasn't it fortunate they stayed in their home?
And where was my faith in human goodness?

Elegy for the Northern Flying Squirrel

1

Not exactly a flier but a glider
      between trees,
the squirrel soars by shifting

      her cape, tightening
and loosening the parachute that stretches
      from ankle to small

cartilaginous wrist bones. From Canada to
      the Appalachians,
she seeds, through her scat, the conifer

      forest with spores
of truffle-like fungi the trees require.
      Will anyone notice

the dwindling of unbroken stands
      of spruce and hemlock
that cool off mountain streams?

2

We have words
for this: *fragmentation, disappearance*
     of ecosystems.

Once the cambered airfoil
     of furry tail
stuck an Olympic landing on a trunk.

     We did not witness
or admire the aerobatic, nocturnal feats,
     visible only to other

canopy dwellers and the field biologist.
     But have you seen
the small, wingless insects infesting

     the hemlocks
by your house? The cottony tufts?
     The dying trees?

3

The fast decline of the Northern
Flying Squirrel:
symptom of larger malaise

and contributor
to it. Today you can purchase one
as an exotic pet

at six weeks old and keep it warm
in a pouch you wear
under your shirt between hand feedings,

so that it bonds to
you and learns to come to the human
for comfort and safety.

In Montefiore Cemetery

Although the dying don't want to talk much,
the dead have all the time in the world.

However, a vast indifference has replaced
our old relations. Emporium of headstones!

Since when do you leave old antipathies
mid-sentence? Choose silence over bickering?

Who among you has ever taken
the long view? *Talk to you and talk to the wall*

Bubbe used to say. Just giving me
some of my own medicine? *I'll give you something*

to whine about, father bristled. Now
the only whine comes from a chainsaw

across the street. Whoever thought I'd miss
those dead-end arguments? *So now you want*

to talk, college girl?
                I take my case to Moses
Montefiore, in whose breast the pained cry

of misery and wretchedness found an echo.
He says, *I was a court Jew and a diplomat in my time.*

My advice to you: philanthropy through
planned giving. Volunteer at the Jewish

Home for the Aged. Montefiore, I beseech,
Where is everyone?

Serve a congregation as lavador, washing
and preparing the bodies of the dead for burial.

Think globally, act locally.
Consider those of all creeds brethren.

My dead! I miss you! Won't you give a sign?
Make a joke at my expense?

Silence, Montefiore nods, *is the restraint of wisdom.*
No tongue speaks as much ill as one's own.

Our Best Selves

in memory of Miriam Goodman (1938–2008)

Like actors in summer stock
we played our best selves
visiting her rustic cabin.

I lay on the floor in a back
room with the cranky
grandson

and played Candyland
until he went down
for a nap.

Paula played Bach's
cello suites
on the screened porch,

each note a mournful
summons,
orderly, unfolding.

*   *   *

On the dock
with their father
the boys learned

to extract the hook
without tearing
the flesh, to cast

their lines
in a joyous arc.
Leslie swam

across the lake,
her body a rhythmic
voluptuousness,

her steady plashing
a signal to the terrier
ashore. Miriam hailed

and embraced summer
and winter people
in the annual

June convocation
at the beach, updates
and invitations

all around:
they could see
she was sick, bewigged,

but she was here,
now, steadying herself
against the piling,

going in slowly,
the burning chill
on her thighs,

on her hips, her waist,
as she studied the familiar
lake, its inlets, pines,

and boulders vivid
as the cabin's manifest,
the list of essential linens

and batteries and cast iron
pots passed on each year—
revised and copied—

for her beloveds.

*   *   *

Grilled vegetables,
beet soup, corn, and nine
of us round the table

pouring and laughing,
stories of the day
taking on their initial

color and flavor
before we cook them
in summer's brine—

misquotes and retellings.
Beneath a full moon,
inside their tent,

the boys undress,
and we see their limbs—
animated cave paintings

against the tent's fabric—
or a shadow play
enacting one summer day.

Scrabble players
assemble at the table.
This year Jules wins

every game, and when
she laughs, her red hair
ripples as it did

when she was ten
and wild as her eldest
awake in his sleeping bag,

looking up at his grandmother's
sky, imagining the salamanders
he'll catch tomorrow.

II

And So Forth

In the last years of his life, my father
concluded every sentence *and so forth.*
Three-syllable glaze, the phrase purveyed
the sweet aftertaste of icing, a hopeful
sufficiency. *I went to the doctor and so forth.*
I pictured him coming about, a sail
tightening to the wind in a graceful
arc, the whole boat of him forthwith gliding.
Never one for details, he'd body forth
with his spasm of sonants—*and so forth*—
shellacking particulars. No solvent
loosened names or dates,
and my mother died before she chose
laziness or cognitive loss. No matter.
Let others blather on with unnecessary hype;
my father made do with his small class
of words. Conjunctions fortified him,
lent him congress and congregation, as in
I had lunch with the boys and so forth,
to which I, blabbermouth daughter,
amend a buoyancy of pastrami and coleslaw.

Rescue Parable

Though saved from starvation and given
his own name, bowl, bed;

though he wears the tags
of ownership and veterinary care;

though he sleeps in the sun with his cat
who grooms him in the autumn afternoon;

he carries every bone to the back of the yard,
digs with his forepaws a grave,

and with his nose, dutiful as one enslaved,
covers with dirt the coming poverty.

The Weight

for Jill Morgan

If some true measure of my mother's
      sorrow lay in each ounce of vermeil and gold,
then I could, bracelet by bracelet,
      account for years of sadness,

and so I took the box
      to the floor, to hold and smell
each piece, invoking the plate glass jeweler's
      windows and then the jolt of possession

when my father pointed to a ring or
      necklace pinned to a velvety cushion.
Sometimes, aboard a cruise ship, he'd get the urge;
      sometimes, flushed, after winning at the track.

She never went for the most expensive
      things like some girls do, he said after she died.
I sat there, cupping in my palms the stories,
      my hands sinking with the weight.

Her Lies

Carpenter bees continue to pock
the fascia boards, drill the wood
into runnels of connecting troughs.

Humming above me, they debride
the gallery, disappear inside.

They say these bees can hollow out a house
before anyone comprehends the tiny
piles of dust, almost invisible, on the floor.

Repair

More stall than store, his cramped space on Carmine
smelled of Cat's Paw leather cream polish.
A belt, a boot, our shoes for soles: he restored
them, mended your silver heron lamp
from Norway, replaced your cracked crystal.
He charged so little I wondered how

he paid the rent, a Chekhov character
transposed to the West Village, resolving
toggle switches, latches, sundered bolts,
talking to himself in Russian—jeweler's
loupe fixed to his face.

After the towers fell, the shoe and watch
man moved; what we couldn't repair
between us stayed broken.

Seasonal vendors hawked fir and spruce wreaths.
A mercantile buzz dizzied
Carmine, where windows of valentines surfaced
and disappeared. *In restauro* read the sign,
that spring, on the Church of the Sacred Conversation.

I missed our magician of the material,
tried to bring you renovated things
from the Used CD Emporium
and Bookstore, bazaar of second and third
chances, our New York beyond repair.

The Middle Path

Oh, I am happy to wake and study
my neighbor on his porch swing
stroking his cat and watching the robins
drop to his lawn for the bread he scatters.
A sedentary man with an ailing son,
he has affixed to his three white vehicles
the insignia of the Polish Republic:
predatory bird against a red background,
wings spread to intimidate.
Oh, I am content to visit him at Xmas,
dressed as a dominatrix, with a tin
of homemade ginger cookies, my girlfriend
sporting a tuxedo and topper.
And, I am happy to think back
to my former therapist who brought
her Airedale to our sessions in the brick
and stately mansion outside Cambridge, Mass.
One day she and her dog fell asleep.

I praise my pothead pals who refuse
to accept the rhetoric of the middle path
or ban the forbidden, sweet-smelling joint
after the poached salmon and baby greens.
How can I neglect to celebrate the women
who chose each other and then had children?
Bar Mitzvah invitations come each year,
since all my friends had sons, of the sort
we couldn't find to save our lives.
We saved ourselves instead.
                              Which brings me to
this certain age, this mortgage application,
this recycling bin, this ferry reservation.

Though I contrive to empty out my life,
I can't contain my own enthusiasms
or figure out how I became what my mother
called *a person with too much time on her
hands*, brooding about running out of time.

Understory

for Eloise Klein Healy and Colleen Rooney

I woke to howler monkeys screaming at dawn.
The false-eyed iguana changed from orange to green.

In the raftered lobby, a teal-winged macaw
screeched *hello baby* and the Jesus

lizard ran across the infinity pool
that met the sky. The deceptive cadence

of Bach's Passacaglia and Fugue in C minor
rang in my headphones in the forest

that made its own clouds and thus continually wept.
Del Monte pineapples flanked the road to Tortuguero

where the forbidden Caribbean sparkled with sharks.
In the mangrove, a fallen tree opened its mouth,

turned caiman, and leaves doubled in size every day
above a chevroned tiger heron wading in the slough.

I beached the kayak below tiered and pedestaled
trees festooned in droplets, trees studded with pink

epiphytes, their holdfasts strong as barbed wire.
After a brief fracas with bullet ants and poison

frogs, I revived at the thatched tiki bar
and added a gray-headed kite to my life

list beneath boa constrictor and sloth.
Seven years together, now we no longer speak.

The rainforest absorbs decay in a lyric.
Like a bird in a mist net, the half-life of betrayal.

Xenia

for Leslie Lawrence

Most days that summer your old dog came up,
in the searing heat, with a failing heart,
from your place, the half-mile uphill to mine—

up the steep rise, past the pastured goats, on
the buggy trail that swerves through blueberries.

As you pointed out, *The Odyssey*
is full of tears, everyone weeping
to find and lose and find each other again.

Spent, he struggled the last two hundred yards,
ears low, chest heaving. Hearing
the jangling of his tags I knew the gods

had chosen me to praise him for his journey,
offer food and water, a place to sleep.

Harriers

For a week, the grandeur and mass of palace
      façades sloshed in the waters of the Grand Canal,
            our happiness fugitive as the ornate, shifting

balustrades: oblique, partial. Column, cornice,
      and fluted pilaster dissolved in wet washes,
            reappeared as stone basilicas when we looked back.

Our sham Thanksgiving—pasta, on Murano—
      a glassblower said, *Watch out for Chinese imports*
            in island shops. Next morning, she wanted time

to herself. I copied Tintoretto's *Creation*
      of the Animals: above bright swordfish and pike,
            pairs of marsh harriers and herons flock west with God.

Unspeaking, we toured secret synagogues disguised
      as apartments, adjoining treacherous guilds,
            and returned to the hotel through alleys where men

opened duffels onto counterfeit Prada bags,
      identical to those in dressed windows.
            She bought two for herself; he vanished

into a Baroque wall. At customs, we had little to declare,
      one fraudulent strap loosed from its cheap
            metal ring, the other, like us, coming apart.

Wearing Mother's High School Ring

I

Her maiden name, etched in the ring, means *wine*
merchant in Yiddish, so I toast

her inaugural self—
arching and graceful as maiden grass,

a filly who hasn't won a race but carries
the gene for heart and mildness, the middle,

dutiful child of three, the peacemaker,
translating from Yiddish for little Bubbe

upstairs. When Germany fires on the Polish
army at Danzig, when Gandhi starts a hunger

strike protesting British rule, she's eighteen,
walking the boardwalk in Atlantic City

with the man I found on Ancestry.com.

II

Because I want to think that she felt joy,
because she will marry my father

nine years after the annulment,
I choose her senior year, 1939.

This blond, Jewish, Lithuanian boy
with the great body takes her to the prom.

She wears the Olney High onyx and gold
class ring on a slender finger. He likes

to dance, so she complies. Self-consciousness
usually cripples her but not tonight,

not tonight, oh please! Let her find her voice
like Marian Anderson, denied a concert hall,

singing outside to 75,000 at the Lincoln Memorial.

III

Let's leave her in Fralinger's, on the boardwalk,
buying salt water taffy to take home.

I take her guy aside, ask him, *What makes*
her happy? What music does she like?

Where in the world would she like to go?
And you, Mr. X! Why do you love her?

We've got the rest of our lives to be sad,
he says. *I'm teaching her to drive a car.*

After the World's Fair, we'll go to the Bronx,
listen to Lou Gehrig, the luckiest man alive.

Listen. It's going to get bad. Jews living in
occupied Poland will transfer to ghettos.

On the radio, Billie Holiday sings "Strange Fruit."

IV

She wakes to the headline: *U.S. Denies*
Access to Jewish Refugees. She knows

it's going to get bad. In love, she wants
a home of their own, war jobs to fund

new lives. She still believes it's possible
to dream big dreams, and I would leave her there

with that belief, twirling the high school ring,
spinning before the mirror in her room,

a tomboyish beauty with no knowledge
yet of crematoria and the Neutrality Act

Franklin Roosevelt will advocate.
The Wizard of Oz hits Philly theaters

and "Over the Rainbow" makes the charts.

The Sounds of Yiddish

splat like *matzoh* broken and dropped
in the egg-milk mix for *matzohbrei.*

They knock you deep in the *kishkes.*
They smart—*kine ahora*—with the *schtick* of the canny

mensch who knows *schlock* when she sees it.
You think I'm a *pischer*? Don't *drey mir kop.*

Yiddish knows an example is not proof,
gives a *tumler* with a *pisk* the barbed shrug.

When a schlimazel sells an umbrella the sun comes out.
You should grow like an onion with your head

in the ground. Yiddish hisses with chicken *schmaltz*
sizzling for *knishes.* Not invited to the luncheon?

Don't worry; her *knaidlach* don't float.
Like the Sami with many words for snow,

we have many for *fool. Shtunk. Schlepper. Schlemiel.*
Shmuck. Hear that rumbling across Ukraine?

Yiddish ran from a posse of hazards when
my Bubbe left her *shtetl,* Russians at her back

and a mongrel, Middle High German in her mouth.
A language is a dialect with an army and a navy

the saying goes. To which my peasant relatives reply,
Spare us what we can learn to endure.

Rescue Riddle

When she takes her morning tea, he settles
beside her—body of law and praise,
procuress, his winter and summer hearth.

Each day, to work, she turns her back
on his slim muzzle, narrow rib cage,
small paws braced. She might have left

him to starve with his brothers years ago
on that beach in Mexico, one leave-taking
instead of the thousands ahead of them.

Divers

Dominican Republic

In our gear we circled the dying reef—
gray pillar and star, algal blooms choking
embroidered brain coral come to grief

and rubble. Purple sea fans blew beneath
domed colonies, silken nets floating.
In our gear we circled the sickened reef

depleted by carbon sink and bleached
by rising temperatures. We spoke in
sign, pointed shriveled fingers to griefs

incised, grooved, silted over. Angels leached
from caverns; we followed remote in-
lets where a brittle darkness shingling the reef

housed a school of blue tang that breached
the gloom. A pair of ocean sturgeon smote
my mask in the doomed, ultraviolet light of grief

that lit wrasse, spotted damselfish, and sweep.
When a goatfish jackknifed from the slope
I shuddered with hope for the sessile reef—
and surfaced with my human griefs.

False Summit

Lovers climbed the ridge
past tree line and hail.
When they reached the top

they realized the true
summit lay ahead of them,
a notch in a cloud.

One decided to turn back.
The other continued up the trail.
Who took the wise path?

Each one cried, *She left me
to make my way, alone.*

III

Taking Down the Sculptor's Horse

for Wendy Klemperer

With a blowtorch she burned off the tail
and then the ears and forelock

to weld them later
after transport

We foundered with the chain-fall
until she got a purchase

on the coiled rebar
at the withers

Leslie swore the metal horse breathed
before the winch

reaved it into the air
where it swayed

in a tangent, equine
counterpoise   Then hands

at the mane, haunch,
pastern, and throatlatch

lowered and strapped
the steel creature down

with ratchet and cam buckle
beside the portable generator

into the flatbed
as into the excavator's hollow

or a stall of chiseled wood shavings
for the horn of the hoof

Legacy Children

From the leather seat of the eighteenth-century
        carriage that carried the childhoods of my friend
and her brothers to a castle in the Dordogne—
        where, with their parents, they carved and painted
Belgian draft horses and wrote droll plays
        in which they starred, wearing plumed costumes
        pillaged from the family's steamer trunks—

I understood that my parents did not burden me
        with selling or keeping the mead hall.
No, the Florida condo sold quickly, also the Cadillac.
        They did not leave me in thrall to a troupe
of siblings, including itinerant Henry, the handsome
        farrier, enormous and beloved in the Northeast
        Kingdom for his way with a difficult steed.

No, my parents did not leave me a hunger
        for relations made fantastical in childhood
and thus forever. Or, with a 1000-piece, painted, cast-iron Swiss
        circus for which the children baked clay figurines
in the great room's stove, and where, from the ceiling,
        hung a five-foot replica of the Santa Maria
        with cherry wood masts and hand-sewn sails

which the family employed in sea narrative
        dramas of transatlantic disaster.
My parents gave me a sister, but she took her life,
        confirming griefs we couldn't disable.
They gave me the code to punch for escape, the humble
        Quakers, their accidental feminism, their refusals.
        My shot at happiness? Outsourcing myself to strangers.

How will my friend dispose of the banked barn
        that holds the carriage and the Alps? The thrill
of opening nights and toasts and cast parties?
        The forest where they rode to the hounds—
mother in the lead, father in the rear?
        If she abandons it, where will she go?
        And will she find me when she arrives there?

Dog Person

Like burdocks, loyalty attaches to her.

Will get quilled or skunked
without learning a thing about character—

when threatened, she bites.
When bitten, she recoils.

Traveling by automobile, she prefers
a front seat.

Surpasses her peers in agility and execution.

Leashed, she pulls.
Freed, she heels.

Lavishes attention on beloveds
upon whom she sits and boldly kisses.

She selects from her basket a sequence
of oddments and returns them one by one.

Although she may become obsessed
with one thing or another,

she excels in neatness.

Sailing, she sports a blue-and-white
bandana and takes the stern.

Will repeatedly try to rescue a dummy.

The Civil War Comes to Town

What could I say to the 128th Pennsylvania
Infantry Regiment reenactor,
pouring coffee by the Company C fire
with his sons? *Have some bacon*, he offered,
gesturing to the iron pot, blackened
by the 1863 campaigns—Chancellorsville
and Wapping Heights, Auburn Mills and Kelly's Ford.

We followed behind after father, one
costumed boy offered. Then he ran off
with his wooden rifle to shoot his brother.
My dog lay down in the sun. *Now we've got
a Company mutt*, one blue-suited soldier said.
I stood by the chess board, watching the soldiers
mull over their moves. *We mustered in August*

of 1862, my reenactor told me. *Coffee?*
They offered me a seat at the writing table
where a recruit struggled with a letter
to Po River, Virginia, May 10, 1864.
Inside the tent, someone hemmed a coat,
pulling the needle through coarse, blue wool.
Young men rubbed Huberd's Shoe Grease on brogans,

and soon I fell to mending blankets.
I stuffed my hair into a cap and took
the role of Rob, cross-dressing scout who saved
three hundred souls. Thus, I joined the men
of Company C; we nursed our sick
without women or running water;
bayonets ready, we entered the enemy's tents.

Threesome Interval

That summer my cooking exceeded
      all expectations.
I excelled in tagine of chicken with olives
      and a curried Thai soup.

We biked to yoga at six a.m.,
      biked home virtuous
and clarified. Was it the Prozac? The new
      puppy glorious in red curls?

Your new man, the Scrabble champ? Even
      the wild blueberries astonished.
In Shelburne Falls, from the viewing platform
      we admired the glacial potholes

ground from granite by snowmelt and gyrating
      stone. Swirls marbled
the rock with a natural patina. We kept
      our composure,

despite hundreds of millions of years
      of whirlpooling abrasion.
Arriving at the Walt Whitman party, in great spirits,
      I wondered: might we try a trip to Rome?

At the tag sale, he found a first edition
      of Frost, and you snagged
a Henckels knife. We didn't deserve such
      good luck, but luck found us anyway.

The Dog I Didn't Want

ran in anxious circles around the room—
stacked crates of dogs in need of homes.

I drifted toward a puppy, nonchalant;
the assistant said he hadn't, yet, been fixed,
and returned the dog I didn't want to his cage.

An older couple, looking to assuage
a recent loss, sat with a spaniel, transfixed.
The dog I didn't want yipped and cried

in his metal pen. "Take him for a walk,"
the keeper called, gave me a leash. Outside he stalked
the mailbox post and tugged to come inside.

He wouldn't meet my gaze or lick my hand
or charm with any doggy gifts. Instead,
the dog I didn't want curled up and tucked his head

into the coiled spiral of his body, color of sand.
Quiet, eyes closed, snout down, he awaited his fate
like one bound for the gallows or the chair.

Resigned, unloved, the dog I didn't want
in his despair won me his small estate.

Mushrooms

Given the little I know about mushrooms,
I never should have soaked and sautéed
and eaten the three yellow morels

I picked roadside last May. With spores
in the pits of their honeycombed heads
they had the brainy appearance I trusted.

Twice, in the same remote spot in the woods,
my friend locates a clustered mass of gray-
brown caps—choice Hen of the Woods—beneath leaves.

At eighty-eight, a lover of telling
false from true, she crouches to rub the spoon-
shaped caps, to confirm her sense of things.

The Island
for Suzy Colt

When algae and a mucky haze
      fevered the pond
my friends bought an island,

anchored it 500 yards out—a natural
      water filter the size
of the dining table. Festooned

with iris and wild strawberries,
      the floating scape's roots grew
down through substrate,

fed on the water's nutrients.
      Within a year, microbes rid the pond
of phosphates; the water cleared

and tadpoles buzzed the shore in troops.
      I loved the hydroponic
country's culture and swam

close enough to touch its tiny gardens—
      reed beds and bluebells,
cattails and migratory insects.

Last summer we toweled off and,
      side by side, stared at the floating
wetland nursery. I can't remember

who said what but I know we talked
      about the island,
breathing into the water year after year.

Dyke

The word came after me, then hid each time
I turned to look at it.
It breathed in the hedge. I could hear it bite
and snap the air.

I feared the woman with slicked-back hair
sitting on a bar stool,
her back to the dance floor, a beer in her hands.
Disco drove the word away

but it came back: *Bulldyke, Bulldagger.*
What did the word want
with me, and why this dread, this desire, this
dangerous butch

striding through Kenmore Square
uncamouflaged?
Dyke had a spike in it, a cleated surge.
In leathers, the word leapt

eighteenth-century grillwork
on the Boston Common and led the parade
around the city,
the slow, snaking, joyful motorcade

of a new millennium. First
I had to hate her;
then I had to hurt her; the rest of my life,
I ate from her hand.

When You Look at the Spines of Your Books
for Amy Lang

arrayed around the rooms
you know who you are
as the diver knows herself
by the molecules of air
and water she displaces
carving her torso into form.

The typefaces and shiny patinas
where your fingers rubbed
the titles; the classrooms, the students,
the decades of civil strife;
here, demonstrators still chant and march.
Arguments take shape and you

draft a proposal, you protest in D.C.
When you look at the spines of your books
you know the arduous training of the mind
for clarity and compassion. You are Buddhist
and Hindu, Arab and Jew forever
having to learn the other,

shared climate and history of human
settlement, where alluvial sediment
preserved the striped clay fragments of a flute,
and the ethnographer recorded that
everyone for five hundred miles
knew the harmonies.

Holiday

We slept and woke to the sound of rhythmic surf.
Across the room, my friend lay with her book;
I listened to the spacious hour, its humane breath
on the room, grown large with distant water.

In that monastic calm we took ourselves
lightly, rose and ate, walked the half moon
beach and indulged our ankles with bracelets
of kelp. Underwater, the day kept flut-

tering open, fluttering open—
banded butterfly with its eye-concealing stripe,
blue angel nibbling on a sponge—
and then the boatman put his back to the reef

and returned us to shore, where the afternoon
waited palmate, rinsed, thatch-roofed.
Day moon overhead, we played chess,
long, quiet games, and napped below giant fronds

that fanned us and whispered *easy, easy,*
the way you soothe a high-strung mare, so she
can drop her head and graze on a long lead—
so slack she thinks the groom has set her free.

Listening to Bach on Rt. 89

In a humidity of Baroque proportions
I compose the faces of my friends,
the interweaving themes of our lives.

Banked barn, borscht from garden beets,
the dogs' extravagant greetings
play in counterpoint

to highway berm, median strip, loosestrife—
classic elements of a summer's drive
to visit. Such joyful improvisations!

The Plum Tree
for Carolyn Sachs

Like Shiva, many-armed, already ancient
when my friend bought the place,

        the tree's cracked limbs clawed the air, where
nine feeders hosted generations—noisy

chickadee and siskin, nuthatch and woodpecker.
        Desiccated, unyielding, in spring the tree drew

        indigo bunting and grosbeak to its withering.
Year after year, she could not bear

        to cut it down.
When a sharp-shinned hunted from a wire,

        the farmyard emptied, feeders like out-of-season
ornaments decorating a leaflessness.

One year, thin saplings rose around the great
dead tree, celebrants about a maypole,

        and the sweet scent
of blossoming returned

in the miniature plum trees the birds seeded.
        Young keepers of the temple fire,

        garlanded in white, they circled
the goddess-tree, their fallen petals

marking a sacred wheel, within which
        the dead cede ground to the living.

Provisioned

The goatherd shouldered a mile of wire fence
and strode up the mowing—

                              in their makeshift
pen, brown-hooded, his Boer goats faced
north to follow his progress—
                              where he drafted

a meadow, laying a circular grid
of solar-powered line.

                    All summer I watched
him work, setting his field over the field,

twenty goats grazing wind-driven florets
to reveal the granite below, starting

on a distant rise and clearing again
the sapling-threaded
                    and stone-filled pasture.

Once we spoke. I asked after the goat
with the pendulous
                    sack at her throat.

She has no pain, he said, *so she can live
out her life.*
                    Sometimes goats will isolate
a weak one, but they accept her.

By midsummer the goats know the sound
          of my voice, the shape of my dog and come

to the fence line when I walk the matted trail.

At night I shine my headlamp on the flock.

Some sleep in pairs, their backward-curling horns
        safely angled away from tender flanks.

I scan the portable loggia for
the goitered one
                and find her browsing August

brush with a companion. Soon the goatherd
will coax them across the footpath
                                to commence

the southern face—setting the field over the field
to reveal the field beneath.

Acknowledgments

I thank the editors of the following publications in which these poems, some in different versions, appeared:

American Poetry Review: "And So Forth," "Dog Person," "Dyke," "Elegy for the Northern Flying Squirrel," "Her Lies," "Herself," "In Montefiore Cemetery," "Late June Owl," "Our Best Selves," "The Sounds of Yiddish," "Understory," "Wearing Mother's High School Ring,"; *BigCityLit.com*: "A Last Go" as "A Last Go at Pleasure," "Listening to Bach on Rte. 89"; *Poet Lore*: "The Weight"; *Prairie Schooner*: "Divers," "Holiday," "Hospice," "Old Florida," "Prairie Dogs," "Repair," "Rescue Parable," "Storm King," "Sculpture Park," "The Plum Tree," "Harriers" as "Venetian"; *Slate*: "Xenia."

"Kouros" appeared in the *Massachusetts Review*, volume 49, numbers 1 and 2.

"When You Look at the Spines of Your Books" appeared in *upstreet*, number 9 (Ledgetop Publishing, 2013).

For a sabbatical during which I wrote many of these poems, I thank the College of Liberal Arts at the Pennsylvania State University. I thank the Helene Wurlitzer Foundation of New Mexico for a residency grant in Taos. Thanks to Phyllis Hotch for the casita on the mesa and to Frankie B. and Harvey Tolman for the cabin on the mowing. For their reading and counsel on the manuscript, I thank Julie Abraham, James Brasfield, John Daniels, Sally Greenberg, Eloise Klein Healy, Charlotte Holmes, Maren Hubbard, Merrill Kaitz, Susanna Kaysen, Leslie Lawrence, Amy Lang, Khyber Oser, Carolyn Sachs, and Marianne Weil.